HOW TO INVEST
IN SHARES

Books that inspire, educate & empower you to be an investor in company shares

Delivered with honesty, passion and written from personal experience in simple, jargon-free English.

Whether you want to take personal control of your own investments, cut out the expensive middle-men, put your hard-earned cash to better use, save for a long-term dream project, develop a passive income, retire early or grow your life savings faster and stronger while you are still young enough to enjoy the results!

How To Invest In Shares understands that you are smarter than the Financial Services industry thinks you are. You don't have to be dependent on their expensive, self-centred, mostly poor advice. You can make your own investment decisions and achieve far better results. We show you how.

For more information on our products and services or to contact us, visit:

http://www.HowToInvestInShares.co.uk

http://www.SharesCoach.com

HOW TO INVEST
IN SHARES

THE QUICK START GUIDE TO BUYING, SELLING AND INVESTING IN SHARES

ADRIAN BOTHAM

How To Invest In Shares

Version 1.05

ISBN 9781470110888

The right of Adrian Botham to be identified as the author of this work has been asserted by him in accordance with the Copyright, Designs and Patents Act 1988.

Cover and interior text design by Adrian Botham
Graphic Images supplied by Create Space
Visit the author's website: http://www.HowToInvestInShares.co.uk

DEDICATIONS

This is my first book and is dedicated to:

My mum, Sandra, without whom I would not have had the chance in life to become the person that I have become and to achieve the things that I have.

My late Dad, Paul, who encouraged me to do more with my life, embrace it, take my opportunities head-on and celebrate the results. I still hear him saying to me "that's the joy of the open road, boy" on a regular basis.

My late sister, Ferne, who taught me that life is for living, having lots of fun and enjoying myself. Her spirit lives on in the way that I do things, the reason I do them and the decisions I make.

My wife, Lynn, for her love, support and encouragement and for sharing my life journey, wherever it is taking us!

Adrian Botham

August 2012

CONTENTS

TABLES

1 HOW TO USE THIS BOOK

So you want to become a share investor? But you're not sure where to start? Well, I'm here to tell you that you are not alone – and you are off to an ideal start!

This book has been put together by a private investor with more than 27 years of experience investing in shares – someone who started with no knowledge in the subject whatsoever. Someone just like you maybe? Since then, there has been 27+ years of investing and learning!

Having been exactly where you are many years ago, I fully understand how daunting the task can feel when you are starting at the beginning of the learning curve and there is a lot to learn. But I also believe that most books, blogs and training courses make it all seem a lot more complicated than it really is whilst promising you riches beyond your wildest dreams. In my experience, life is not like that but I wish it were!

The other problem you will have reading other people's books is that they are written by ex-city types and accountant-types and so they are full of financial and stock broking jargon. I can promise that you won't get any of that from me!

Yes, I understand a lot of the jargon these days, enough to have proper conversations with Chief Executives of FTSE 100 companies anyway. But I didn't know it when I started out and you will pick some of it up too as you go along. The point that I am trying to make is that it is not necessary to wait until you understand all the jargon before you start investing in shares. It is better to start carefully and build up your knowledge and confidence as you go along.

This short book is intended as an introduction to investing in shares and covers the things you need to consider up front, before investing any of your hard-earned cash in shares. It will help you make some key decisions and start out safely on your own journey to becoming a successful investor.

This book will also ensure that when you do buy your first shares, you get to keep more of the profits for yourself. It even provides you with an outline of a 10-step share buying process, which you can follow every time you buy new shares.

I hope you find it useful and that it inspires you to make a start.

Happy investing!

2 WHAT IS INVESTING?

Investing is a word that is used an awful lot. Sometimes it is used correctly and other times it is abused. For example, how many times have you heard a salesperson talking about "investing in a new car" or "investing in a new coat", for example?

Before we go any further then, it is important to define what we mean by investing. One definition that sums it up for me, quite succinctly, is the one given in The Chambers English Dictionary, which defines investing as "laying out for profit".

Now, straight away, we can see that true investing is not the same as buying. *Buying* is about spending money or "laying out" on a product or service, not necessarily with the intention of making a profit. Investing, on the other hand, is the deliberate activity of buying something, an asset, with the expectation of making a profit during our ownership of that asset.

Similarly, investing is not the same as saving either, for three principle reasons. *Saving* involves setting money aside in a safe place until some time later when we might need it or decide what we want to spend it on. Saving is therefore a passive activity, not a deliberate activity.

Saving is also more about holding on to what we already have than it is about making a profit from what we have. In other words, it is focused on asset maintenance rather than asset growth. Finally, saving does not involve "laying out" on anything because we expect to get it all back at some point in the future.

In days gone by, people used to save their money by putting it under the mattress or storing it in a biscuit tin in the kitchen! This is much easier to understand than modern methods of putting your money into a bank account because we expect to earn interest on our bank savings which we never used to receive from the mattress or the biscuit tin. This earning of interest is probably the reason why lots of people confuse saving with investing.

Investing is more risky than saving because there is a chance that the asset we buy will fall in value during our ownership. For this reason, investing is often viewed by some as "a bit of a gamble" and thus confused with gambling, although it is easy to see why.

Gambling is a game of chance where a bet or wager is made on a particular outcome and the probability of losing your stake money is higher than the probability of winning – usually in a big way! Yes, I know, this seems to describe investing. However, gambling does not involve the ownership of any assets in the way that investing does.

In summary then, investing is a deliberate activity, involving laying out a sum of cash, on the purchase of an asset, with the expectation of making a profit from owning the asset, although there is always a risk that the asset you purchase will depreciate in value instead of making you a profit.

Still want to be an investor? I've not frightened you off? Good, because most people need to be investors!

3 ARE YOU READY TO INVEST?

Are you ready to invest? "YES" I hear you cry! But wait a minute – investing is a risky activity as I've already explained. So you should never invest money that you cannot afford to lose. That means putting your finances in order first.

1) *Bills and regular spending*. Make sure you know that you have sufficient income to cover your on-going spending including regular savings e.g. for holidays, Christmas, etc.

This involves getting your spending under control and living within your means i.e. making sure that your income exceeds your expenses every month. By doing so, you will always have some spare cash left over each month that you can do something positive with.

2) *Clear your debts*. If you have spare cash, the best thing you can do with it is pay off any non-mortgage debts that you have including credit cards, car loans, other personal loans, etc.

The rate of interest on such debts (and thus the savings you can make by paying them off) is often higher than the returns you can expect to make from regular investments so it makes perfect sense to clear these first. In other words, what is the point in risking your money to make a return on shares of 8%, say, if you can save 20% interest by paying off your monthly credit card bill?

When you have your personal non-mortgage debts paid off or if you are frugal enough not to have any to start with, then you are ready for step 3.

3) *Emergency cash fund*. You never know when you might need it for a new car, house repairs, new washing machine, new job, new spouse, whatever! So make sure you have cash savings of at least 3 months salary tucked away in a cash savings account at the bank, paying a decent rate of interest. Ideally, you should consider having 6 months of cash tucked away if you can.

When you have completed steps 1 to 3 above, you will have developed a much greater awareness of your personal finances and have hopefully developed ways to reduce your spending further to free up some cash each month for investing.

Well done!

It's now time to learn how to become an investor!

4 YOUR REASONS FOR INVESTING?

The first step to becoming an investor is to understand your own personal objectives. So, the key question you must ask yourself is:

"Why do I want to invest?"

Most people will want to be an investor at some point in their lives but their reasons for doing so will be different. The most popular reason that people invest is for their **retirement** i.e. their ***long-term future***.

Retirement planning is not everyone's cup of tea and very few people understand retirement accounts or pensions. It is normally a good idea to have one of these things principally because you may be able to get FREE money from your employer matching your contributions or from the Government allowing you to contribute pre-tax income and make tax-free gains.

Other special accounts may not allow you tax-free contributions but they will allow tax-free gains and tax-free withdrawals instead. Whether you pay tax on the way in or on the way out (you will have to do one or the other) is a personal choice driven by the type of account you choose, which should in turn be driven by your own personal circumstances now and when you retire.

The other thing to remember though is that retirement accounts and pensions are highly regulated products, with lots of rules attached and managed by Governments and insurance companies on your behalf. This means that they restrict how much money you can put in tax-free, when you can get it out again, how much you can take out as a lump sum and when you have to spend the rest on an annuity to convert the fund into an income stream.

So, whilst they have their uses, there is no law that says you have to put all your eggs into the one basket. Starting your own share portfolio is much more flexible and has many long-term uses, apart from funding fun and games in your retirement.

Another good reason why you might want to start investing is because you may want the money for something in the future, even though you don't know what that something is yet! We all have **dreams** right? What is it that you dream of? Do you dream of having a nice big house in the country or by the beach one day? Do you want to go on a trip or adventure of a lifetime? Do you want to quit your job and retire early?

Investing in shares can help you to build a *passive income* (to be precise it is a portfolio income but that is splitting hairs) by which I mean a way of generating an income which does not involve you working as an employee or in a business of your own. The beauty of it is that other people will be working to generate the income for you whilst you put your feet up! How cool is that?

Another trigger point for people wanting to invest is when they have their *first child*. Thoughts turn to education fees, paying for weddings, helping them buy their first car or property, etc. If you don't have or want children you may still want to *save long-term* for similar activities such as your own education, your first property, a second property as a holiday home, or whatever.

Talking of *saving*, more and more these days, with cash savings accounts paying such little interest, you might just be looking for higher investment returns to put your money to good use. As long as the time period involved is *for a minimum of ten years*, share investing could be appropriate for you.

It is also a fact that most people usually come into some money at some point in their lives. So you may have inherited *a lump sum* from a rich relative or received a redundancy package? Maybe you have received a divorce settlement from a rich spouse? Or sold a business? If you are really lucky – you might have won the lottery! No? Well, whatever the source of your lump sum, you will want to invest it wisely and investing some of it in shares could be a good thing to do after paying off your debts, setting aside an emergency fund and making sure you have enough to live on. Oh, and spent a little bit of it on treats for you and yours!

Whatever your reasons for investing, it is vitally important that you are clear on your own objectives because you need to know how much risk you are prepared to take with your cash. Share investing is not for everyone but being able to sleep at night is!

5 WHAT ARE SHARES?

So you have some spare cash to invest - what now?

There are several things you could do with it. Rather than just diving into shares and then regretting it later (probably) it is worth considering the other alternatives first:

1) Put it in a *savings* account – It'll be safe there, probably, however that is saving, not investing and you should already have an emergency cash fund

established in a savings account. So you can afford to be a bit more adventurous with any additional cash that you have created for investing purposes.

2) Put it into *Fixed-Term Bonds* – In the UK these are often confused with bank savings accounts but they are not the same. In the US, they are called *Certificates of Deposit* (CD), which is a term I like much better. They are different to bank savings accounts because you lock up your money for a fixed period of time that you agree with the bank at the outset.

So, for example, you can arrange these for 1, 2, 3, 4 or 5 years, say, and you are not allowed to withdraw your money during that time. Your reward for loaning your money to the bank in this way is a higher rate of interest than you would obtain from a similar savings account. That's because the bank is able to lend your money to someone else (to make money for themselves from it) secure in the knowledge that you won't want it back until the end of the agreed term. If you do ask for it back, you will have to close your account and you will be penalised by losing interest previously earned.

3) Buy *Government Bonds* – Also a safe home, usually involving "loaning" your money to the Government for a period of 3 or 5 years, after which you get your money back with interest. Interest can be at a fixed rate or linked to, say, inflation. If you are a low risk investor, this could be a good option, but returns are low to reflect the safety benefits. It is the Government remember!

4) Buy *Corporate Bonds* – Similar to Government Bonds except a Company, not the Government, issues them. Hence they are higher risk but usually pay a higher rate of interest as a result. The price of the bonds can also go up or down in value so we could make a gain or loss when we sell them. Or the company could go bust and we could lose our investment! Unlikely, but it does happen sometimes!

5) Buy a **Property** – This could be a good option if you have a lump sum big enough for a deposit, at least. More than likely you will need to finance a mortgage as well as your deposit, which means having sufficient income from your other activities or tenants occupying the property.

Tenants will need managing, probably via contracts and taking up your time, unless you employ an agency to manage the property and tenants for you, at a cost. Property also incurs high transaction costs when buying and selling. It also needs regular maintenance (more cost) and incurs taxes (yet more cost). Leave it empty and you could find squatters moving in! Okay, enough about property – there's a more flexible option...

6) Invest in **Shares** – These are small pieces of a company, also known as stocks, equities or securities, created to enable the ownership equity of a company to be shared amongst several investors. The ones we are interested in are public

shares, which means they are traded on a stock market and available to members of the public.

This gives us a means of buying and selling shares, finding out what the price (value) of our share holding is at any given time, investing whatever amount we wish, selecting a wide range of companies from a wide range of industries; even from different countries if we wish.

Owning shares in a company therefore means that we own a proportion or percentage of that company. So, if we owned all of the shares of a company, we would own the whole company. This is how public companies get taken over you know, by people buying up all of the shares in the company and then taking the business private i.e. off the public stock exchange.

What I am getting at here is that owning shares allows you to own a part of a business or several parts of several businesses and thus share in the profits of those businesses without doing any work in or for those businesses. That's how you generate your passive income that I mentioned earlier.

   Does that sound good to you?   If shares are for you, then we'll move on.

6 WHY INVEST IN SHARES?

I've already described some of the benefits of shares such as flexibility, ease of valuation, availability, variety, etc. but what about their rates of return? Well, I've saved the best until last!

According to the Barclays Capital Equity Gilt Study, the comparative rates of return for shares, bonds and cash savings (after accounting for inflation) are as follows – what do you notice?

	2010 1yr	Last 10 yrs	Last 20 yrs	Last 50 yrs	Last 111 yrs
Shares	8.9%	0.6%	6.0%	5.4%	5.1%
Corp. Bonds	3.9%	2.1%	N/A	N/A	N/A
Gov't Bonds	4.4%	2.4%	5.8%	2.5%	1.2%
Cash	-4.1%	1.1%	2.6%	1.7%	1.0%

Table 1: Comparative Rates of Return; Source: Barclays

1. Shares performed the worst over the last 10 years - perhaps not surprising given we have had two stock market crashes during this period;

2. Apart from that, shares consistently performed the best;

3. Cash returns are consistently lower than bonds and shares - cash even made a loss during 2010, after accounting for inflation!

4. In 2010, shares were twice as good as bonds;

5. Shares consistently beat cash returns by 2 to 5 times;

6. Shares performed up to 4 times better than bonds;

7. Surprisingly, Government bonds beat corporate bonds, even though experts say it should be the opposite;

Note that this data does not suggest that shares always perform better than cash or bonds. If we looked at annual data, we'd see some big negative numbers for shares because they are more volatile than cash and bonds. In other words, their prices go up and down more.

However, the data shows that shares outperform the alternatives over the longer time periods we are investing for. When you think about it logically, that makes perfect sense because owning shares is about owning pieces of real businesses.

Businesses are the way that entrepreneurs make their money and are the way that non-entrepreneurs, i.e. employees and the self-employed, earn their living too. So businesses are the engines of capital growth, which provide our jobs, incomes, investments and pay taxes for Governments to spend.

Businesses are inherently focused on growth and take years to get started, become successful by developing a formula or system (a business model) and then exploit that approach to generate growth.

Investing in company shares is the way that those of us who can't afford to buy a whole business and don't want to be an entrepreneur, are able to hitch a ride on the back of someone else's efforts.

That sounds good to me. If it sounds good to you too, then we'll continue.

7 DIRECT OR INDIRECT?

You have the choice of investing directly in shares of individual companies or you can invest indirectly via funds, trackers, etc. Under the heading of *funds*, I include all kinds of mutual funds such as Unit Trusts, Open Ended Investment Companies (OEIC), Investment Trusts and Exchange Traded Funds (ETF).

For all of these, you are paying someone else to manage your money for you. You pick the funds and their fund managers use their skill and judgement (sometimes, but not always as you'll see below) to decide which companies, sectors or commodities to invest in. For people who are happy passing responsibility for their investments to their accountant or financial advisor, these can be a good choice. As you've probably guessed, that's not us! We want to make our own choices and funds limit our choices.

Although ETFs are called funds, they work differently to the other types and are relatively new on the private investment scene. Yes, the cash from all investors is pooled into a big pot and used to buy shares, commodities, etc., just like it is for the other types, but the strategy employed by the ETF fund manager is usually to mimic or track something.

For example, ETFs enable you to "invest" in most commodities without buying and holding the commodity itself. For example, if you buy a gold ETF then, yes, sometimes the ETF manager physically buys and holds the gold, but not always, and in any case you never actually hold the gold yourself.

ETFs are therefore best thought of as a ***tracker***, in this example tracking the gold price index. As well as commodity index trackers, there are many other types. Popular ones include market trackers which track a particular stock market index e.g. UK FTSE 100, US S&P 500 or Japanese Nikkei or stock market sectors e.g. Banks or General Retailers.

Trackers work by pooling investor's money and using it to "invest" in a mix of shares to mimic the movement of the tracked index. While these are okay for some people, I'm not a fan of trackers either. That's because they limit our choices again, but worse than that, trackers buy shares of companies that are performing badly - because they have to - because the company is a member of the index being tracked. Why would anyone want to hold shares in badly performing companies? We only want to buy the best!

8 MINIMIZING YOUR CHARGES

Another big reason for disliking funds and trackers is their ***charges***. Funds typically make an initial charge when you first buy them – 5% is typical but can be higher. So for a $1,000 investment, that's $50 just for the privilege of buying. They also charge annually, so they can pay commission to the fund manager – 1.5% is typical but 2.5% or even higher are not uncommon. That's another $15 - $25+ of your $1,000 but can get far higher if your investment increases in value. If your funds grow to $10,000, that will be $150 to $250+

just for looking after them for you. Nice? I don't think so!

An advantage of ETFs and trackers, over other funds, is that they charge lower annual fees, sometimes as low as 0.5% or less, however it is noticeable that these are on the rise and some now charge 1.5% to 2%! So even for ETFs and trackers, you are paying $5 to $20 of your $1,000 when you buy. In contrast, buying UK shares incurs stamp duty of 0.5%, which is only £5 of your £1,000. Even better, buying US or European shares does not incur any stamp duty at all.

The broker (who buys the shares on your behalf) charges commission, which varies depending on which broker you use. I'll cover this in more detail later but these charges have fallen a lot in recent years and are currently around £10 to £12 per on-line transaction in the UK and usually less in the US, say $10 or so. Moreover, these transaction costs are often irrespective of the initial amount – i.e. $10 charge for $1,000 of shares is 1% compared to $10 charge for $50,000 of shares is only 0.02%!

Yeah but what's a few small per cent between friends? Well, look at this table – starting with $1,000 at various rates of interest:

Return	10 yrs	20 yrs	30 yrs	40 yrs	50 yrs
3%	1,344	1,806	2,427	3,262	4,384
4%	1,480	2,191	3,243	4,801	7,107
5%	1,629	2,653	4,322	7,040	11,467
6%	1,791	3,207	5,743	10,286	18,420
7%	1,967	3,870	7,612	14,974	29,457
8%	2,159	4,661	10,063	21,725	46,902
9%	2,367	5,604	13,268	31,409	74,358
10%	2,594	6,727	17,449	45,259	117,391

Table 2: Returns Over Long Periods; Source: Author

Those small percentages can make a big difference over the long-term. How do you fancy losing 5% of $117,391 (which is $5,870) because of the initial charge? How about $43,000 because of a 1% annual fee? I rest my case!

9 TIMING WHEN TO INVEST

When saving cash in a bank account, it doesn't really matter when you deposit and withdraw it – all that matters is the interest rate and whether it is a "notice account". The value of your cash either stays the same or rises – never falls – assuming we ignore the effects of inflation.

Shares are different. Their value changes constantly, up and down, by the second, when the stock market on which they are traded is open for business. That makes them *volatile*.

In an ideal world, you would buy when the share price is low and sell when it is high but there's no sure way of knowing whether the share's price will rise or fall from this point on.

Charting and historical trend analysis can be used to time your investments but that is far too advanced for us yet! Many so-called traders and day traders, in particular, rely purely on graphical charts and the development of specific patterns of share price movements. But this is a bit of a black art and not scientifically proven. Not only that, but if you are buying shares as a long-term investment, the daily and weekly movement of the share price is pretty much irrelevant. Much more relevant is the underlying nature of the business and its future prospects.

As a beginner then, the best way of overcoming volatility and taking the timing risk out of your share purchases is to **_make regular investments_**. So, instead of spending all your spare cash in one go, invest it in smaller pieces. Yes, on some occasions you would have been better off buying a share sooner, but on other occasions you will benefit by waiting. In general, you will be better off by investing on a more regular basis.

When you get more sophisticated, you will be able to analyse companies and their share price history as well as graphical charts and indicators to time your investments better, not like the share traders do, but like long-term investors do. Warren Buffett is a great example of this because he is a long-term investor too!

Of course, you will need access to the data to enable you to do this. There are lots of systems you can buy for this purpose or you can access a myriad of different websites on the Internet, or even the websites of the companies you want to invest in.

10 SHELTERING YOUR INVESTMENTS FROM TAX

I've already mentioned stamp duty, which is a UK tax on share purchases. Well it is not the only tax we have to consider. If your shares rise in price, then *capital gains tax* could be due on the gain. If you receive any dividend income from your shares then *income tax* may be due on those as well, similar to paying income tax on interest from savings.

In the UK, the capital gains tax and most of the income tax can be avoided if your shares are held in an *Individual Savings Account (ISA)*. Most brokers (you'll need one to buy shares) offer ISA accounts. There are certain rules concerning ISA's, which are beyond the scope of this book, but they are a great way of protecting your profits from tax and it's legal as long as you obey the ISA rules!

If you are not a UK tax-payer, then ISA's will not be available to you but there may be similar schemes that you can use in the country where you live, so I use it here as an example.

Alternatively, if your shares are a long-term investment for retirement then there's another great way of reducing your tax bill if you are a UK tax-payer – a *Self Invested Personal Pension (SIPP)*. This is a Personal Pension that you manage yourself rather than via a pension company. Like with funds and trackers mentioned earlier, the charges are a lot lower and you can buy and sell shares as often as you want with the cash held within the SIPP. Like ISAs there are rules that you have to follow and many SIPP providers to choose from.

Again, if you are not a UK tax-payer, then SIPP's will not be available to you but there are probably similar schemes available to you with similar tax advantages.

For example, US taxpayers have a variety of retirement accounts that they can use to minimise tax on their gains and income. Some of these like 401(k) and IRA's allow tax-free contributions and tax-free gains while your money stays in the fund and you pay tax when you withdraw your money during retirement. Other examples such as Roth-401(k) and Roth-IRA are more like the ISA above, in that contributions are after-tax but your withdrawals are free of tax later.

If your share investing is for retirement, wholly or in part, then tax-saving methods such as these should be incorporated into your planning. Tax-free anything is free money! If you have an employer making contributions on your behalf then they may even match any additional contributions you make into your retirement account – more free money!

Hopefully, you have also concluded that with savings accounts, certificates of deposit, bonds, property, etc that I mentioned earlier, all the purchases are with post-tax income and any gains, whether capital or income, are taxed. If you want to be clever with your money, only pay tax when you have to (legally of course) by making full use of all the special accounts and allowances available.

11 OPENING A BROKER ACCOUNT

If you are a complete beginner to share investing, then you will need to open an account with a broker before you can start buying shares.

Before the internet took over our lives, shares were held in the form of a paper **certificate** and the process of buying and selling took several days whilst you waited for certificates in the post, and so on, by which time share prices had changed! In those days, when you were choosing a stockbroker, the only things you had to consider were their fees and whether you wanted their advice of which shares to buy: the alternative being an execution-only service.

Nowadays, there is no need for share certificates (although some people still use them). Shares are best held in *nominee accounts* with a bank. Essentially, these are a lot like regular bank accounts except you have your shares held in them electronically rather than your [electronic] cash. So they are safer (you don't need to store them in a safe place to protect them from burglars or fires at home) and you can trade quicker and easier without all the paperwork.

If you choose to transact your shares on-line via an execution only broker then your fees will be minimised and the broker will provide on-line services to enable you to see your shares in your nominee account. This will enable you to value them, see when you have dividends paid, how much cash is in your nominee account, etc.

In the US, on-line trading can cost as low as $7 although $10 is more typical. Trading by telephone can cost $13 - $35 and broker assisted trading (where you receive advice on what to buy or sell and when) can cost $20 - $45, typically. In the UK, on-line trading is typically £10 - £12 and telephone trading £15 - £25. Trading using old-fashioned certificates always costs more than using nominee accounts as you would expect.

More than likely, your on-line broker will also provide a wealth of research on markets, company shares, historical share price charts, etc. which will help you to do your own analysis and manage your portfolio. Often, these services are free although not always so you need to check. Other things you might want to consider include:

- Which share markets you want to trade with;

- Share trading only or a variety of investment types;

- The kind of research information that is available;

- Ease of using their trading platform;

- Nominee accounts or share certificates;

- Charges for trading and administration fees;

- Availability of tax friendly wrappers (ISAs, SIPPs, IRA or similar) and their charges;

- Etc.

This is not an exhaustive list and it is worth spending some time examining and researching brokers offerings on-line thoroughly before deciding, as there is a wide choice and variety of brokers available. Personally, I would stick with the household names such as well-known banks and established stockbrokers that you have heard of.

Don't necessarily choose the cheapest broker, as security of your money and ease of using the trading platform are arguably more important. If the on-line software is complicated to use, it will start to annoy you after a while and could end up costing you money if you make a mistake by clicking the wrong thing while you are using it!

When you have your account open, you're ready to buy your first shares. Now the fun really starts! And the worry! And the self-doubts! And! And! And!

12 HOW TO BUY YOUR FIRST SHARES

When you have your account open, you are ready to trade and will follow the process below every time you buy a share:

1. Decide on a suitable investment strategy;
2. Find shares that fit your chosen strategy;
3. Do your own research on suitable shares you could buy;
4. Choose a share you want to buy;

5. Establish clear reasons why you want to buy this share;
6. Decide how much money you want to invest in this share;
7. Place a buy order with your broker;
8. Check the correct shares are now in your account;
9. Get all excited about buying your shares;
10. Start worrying about your shares!

Okay, you may be thinking that I am joking about steps 9 and 10? I'm not. I'm speaking from experience. For different people, the period between getting all excited and starting to worry will vary depending on what kind of person you are and whether your shares go up or down after you've bought them.

Steps 9 and 10 are also the main reasons why investors lose money – also known as **emotional attachment**. Other causes of losing money are skipping steps 1, 2 and 3 and starting the process at step 4, usually after reading a share tip in a magazine or share tipping newsletter or listening to a man in a bar!

Step 1 involves deciding your investment strategy, which can be as simple or as complex as you like. At its basic level, it involves deciding whether you want to invest for capital growth (shares rising in price) or income (shares paying dividends). You'll need to consider how much risk you want to take with your money, which industry sectors you would like to invest in, which stock markets you want to trade on, etc. When you are starting out, it is usually best to invest in large blue-chip shares on a recognised stock market like the FTSE 100 or Dow Jones and buy a company that you are familiar with and have plenty of information about.

Step 2 involves identifying shares that match your chosen strategy and narrowing down your search to a short list of shares that you can examine closely. So for example, if you wanted a large blue-chip pharmaceutical stock on the UK FTSE 100, there are three you could choose from. If it is growth you want then you consider all three but if it is income you want then your choice reduces to just two.

In *step 3*, you research those companies using sources of information available to you such as investor pages on the company's website, news sites, etc. until you are ready to narrow your search down to just one share in *step 4*.

Step 5 may seem a bit odd and also another step that you might feel tempted to skip, but don't. It is essential for knowing when to sell your shares later on. Put simply, if you don't know why you bought your shares then how are you going to decide when things have changed and that it is time to sell them? Successful investing is all about making your own decisions and having strong positive reasons for your actions.

Step 6 is a common problem for new share investors, always asking how much they should invest in a share. If this is a problem or question for you then the good news is that it only depends on two things:

Transaction Cost: including the commission charges paid to your broker and any other charges like the UK stamp duty.

Total Investment Amount: that is the amount you have to invest in shares at this time.

To fully understand how these two numbers work together, let's take an example.

If you have $10,000 to invest and it costs $20 in charges every time you buy some shares, then if you invested the whole amount into one share, the costs would represent 0.2% of your investment. In other words, your shares would only need to rise by 0.2% for you to get that transaction cost back. That is good. The downside is that you will have all your money invested in one company. If bad news hits that company, then your investment will take a big hit. So a one-share portfolio is very high risk. It is much better to spread your risk by investing in a variety of company shares in a variety of sectors as soon as you can.

If you used the same $10,000 to buy $500 investments in 20 different companies, you would have a much lower risk portfolio that is much more able to withstand problems should they occur at one of your companies. Of course, you now have investments in 20 companies and so there is more likelihood of a problem occurring in one of them than there would be if you were only invested in one company. However, you'll just have to trust me when I say that the risk to your entire portfolio is lower than in my first example.

However, the real downside of this second example is that, in buying 20 different shares, you have incurred 20 times the transaction costs! Each share investment of $500 has cost you $20 in charges which is 4%. In total, the cost of diversification has cost you 20 x $20 = $400 which equals, of course, 4% of $10,000. This time, your portfolio will need to rise by 4% just to recover your transaction costs. The advantage is that not all of your shares need to rise by 4%; only the combined result needs to be 4%. So some shares could even fall in price, as long as the others compensated by rising much more than 4%.

I hope you are following me on this? What I am trying to say is that deciding how much to invest in any one share is a balancing act between costs and portfolio risk. If you have $5,000 - $10,000 to invest at the beginning, I would recommend investing $1,000 in each share and establishing a portfolio of 5-10 shares.

If you have more than $10,000 to invest, I would start to invest more than $1,000 in each, aiming to establish a portfolio of at least 10 shares and no more than 25. The more shares you have, the more time it takes to monitor, reading news, keeping track of company prospects, etc. and the benefits of diversification diminish rapidly after you have 30 shares in your portfolio.

If you have less than $5,000 to invest, I would recommend you buy fewer shares and add to the portfolio gradually as you have more cash available. This is how I started and, once you get the investment bug, you will be much more driven to save money from other expenses in order to invest it in shares.

So, because of the transaction costs, the minimum I would recommend investing is $500, unless your transaction charges are a lot lower than mine. In any case, you don't want to be relying on your shares to have to increase by more than 5% before you get your money back and don't forget that you incur transaction fees when you sell as well as when you buy. So that $20 now becomes $40 and the amount of gain you need to get your money back now doubles to 8% of $500!

So if money is tight initially, try to save $500 before you start and buy one company's shares with it. Then save another $500 and buy a second company. Build up to 5 shares in your portfolio, then 10 shares. After you get to 10 shares, consider investing more money per share, say $750 or $1,000. As your portfolio grows and you need to keep it at no more than 30 shares, you will need to invest more money in each share, say rising to $2,000, $2,500, $5,000, $10,000 per share as you go.

If all this sounds unlikely and you don't think you will ever get to this position, then don't be so defeatist. Nobody told me about this stuff when I started but it is all perfectly logical when you think about it and it is exactly what I have experienced.

If this all seems complicated, then it probably explains why beginners always have difficulty with working out how much to invest. It is really not as difficult as it sounds. You just need to work out what the percentage of the investment amount is taken up by the costs and try to balance that with the number of shares you are buying. Of course, if you can find a broker with low transaction charges, then you can afford to invest less than $500 each time.

Step 7 involves logging into your on-line broker account or contacting your broker if it is a telephone account and placing your buy instructions. This is a bit scary the first time you do it but is as simple as communicating which share you want to buy, receiving information on how much the shares will cost to buy each (i.e. the price they are trading at right now) and then confirming how many you would like to buy at that price or the total amount of money you want to invest in that share (including or excluding commission charges and stamp duty if it applies). That's it!

In *step 8*, you check to make sure it has all gone through correctly. Oh yes, you may laugh but I am serious. There have been times when I click away on-line and end up with the shares in the wrong trading account or press too many or too few zeroes – it is easily done. So take your time and check everything you do just to make sure.

Documenting all your buy and sell decisions is also to be recommended to assist with your learning. You will make mistakes as well as having successes and looking back over your investment journal will help your analysis of what worked and what didn't.

Better still, don't just learn from your own experiences - learn from others who have already made the mistakes. I don't need to tell you that though, do I, because you are reading this and learning from my mistakes already!

Unless you are made of stone, you will feel a rush of excitement after buying your first shares (**step 9**)! I always do, even now, and I've been investing in shares for the last 25 years. I suppose it is a bit like buying anything for yourself, whether it is the latest gadget, a new pair of shoes or a great new book about "How To Invest In Shares!" Sorry, I couldn't resist that one.

The difference here of course is that you are buying something in the hope that it will make you money in the best way that man ever invented. After doing your work in the researching and buying of this little baby, you are now going to sit back and do nothing more other than to monitor its progress every now and then by following its adventures, exploits and successes in the news as it grows bigger and makes you money. That's if you've picked the right company to invest in, of course.

If you haven't, you will be monitoring its progress only to find that it has gone astray, got involved in things it shouldn't, become involved with people it shouldn't and is losing money rather than making it. Even if these things were not true, you would be inhuman if you did not concern yourself with these possibilities to some degree after the euphoria of buying the shares has worn off and the honeymoon period afterwards is over. This is **step 10** and is a good place to be emotionally, I think, for several reasons.

You will remember this feeling next time that you are researching shares to buy and it will have the effect of engaging you fully in your analysis. It will spur you on to satisfy yourself that the share you are going to buy next is indeed a strong company with great prospects. In other words, it's a bit like having butterflies before presenting or go on stage in front of other people. The time to worry is when you don't feel the butterflies because that is the signal that you don't care anymore about the outcome.

The trick is to not let these concerns or butterflies overwhelm you to the extent that you can't sleep at night. If that happens then share investing may not be for you. Go back to the early pages of this book and make sure that you really are investing money that you can afford to lose. As long as that is the case, then if you follow my guidance and take things steadily, your confidence will build and you will develop a nice share portfolio for the future to realise your objectives and dreams.

13 WHAT TO DO NEXT

Unfortunately, we've come to the end of this book but it is only the start of your investing journey!

I hope you have found the book useful in helping you focus on what is important and that it has inspired you and given you the confidence to start investing in shares.

More information is available via my web sites:

http://www.HowToInvestInShares.co.uk

http://www.SharesCoach.com

The "How To Invest In Shares" website started out life as a blog and is continuously updated with new blog articles on a weekly basis. The website has now matured into a portal, offering free resources and promoting products, training programs, coaching services, stock market analysis tools, etc. to enable new and aspiring investors to get started safely and easily with your stock market shares portfolios.

"SharesCoach.com" provides training programs and private coaching services and is focused exclusively on the subject of investing in shares – how to get started, how to build your portfolio, how to establish your investment strategy and so on.

The coaching services can be utilized alongside the training programs or on their own and are delivered in a variety of formats depending on your budget and required level of personalisation.

Formats include personal coaching via Skype, group coaching via teleseminars or webinars and an innovative low-cost on-line coaching service called *Shares Coach Online.*

Ownership of shares in companies brings about a feeling of involvement in a way that pensions, mutual funds and other investment vehicles will never do. That's because investing in shares brings the opportunity to own a slice of real businesses operating in many industries, markets, environments and countries across the globe like nothing else can.

The sheer act of owning the shares in a particular company arouses your curiosity of that business, its dealings, what it does and its ongoing prospects. Share ownership therefore educates you in many aspects of business, economics, commodities, politics, finance and the world we live in without the need to go to business school.

Not only that, but you will discover that investing in shares is the most flexible and profitable way to build personal wealth and passive income for yourself as long as you do it properly and in an intelligent manner.

This book is the first in a planned series, which together, will form a comprehensive library for beginners to investing. Details will be published via my blog; my newsletter and social media sites so keep a look out for these.

If you have not done so already, you can easily keep in touch with my latest news and articles by signing up to my free email updates via the sign up form on my web site. You can also follow me on my Facebook page, "How To Invest In Shares"; via Twitter @sharescoach or Linkedin via our "How To Invest In Shares" group and company page.

I love to hear your comments regarding your share investing progress, successes, concerns or questions and/or feedback on any of my products or publications – so don't be shy! Contact me and let me know how you're getting on.

I wish you the very best of success with your future investing and the wealth, passive income and financial freedom it brings you.

ABOUT THE AUTHOR

Adrian Botham is a self-taught private investor with more than 27 years of experience in managing his own share portfolio. While still a university student, he realised one of his ambitions - to become a share investor. He bought his first shares in 1985, with £100 left over from his first year student grant, during the UK Government privatisations. Unsure of what he was doing and with no idea how the stock market worked, he bought the shares anyway, believing the best way of learning was by doing!

Since then, Adrian's share portfolio has grown dramatically, along with his knowledge of investing in shares, business, economics and finance. These days, Adrian has a BSc honours degree in Pure Mathematics from Warwick University and a first class Masters degree in Business Administration (MBA) from Bradford University School Of Management among his qualifications.

Adrian believes in adopting a holistic approach to investing - applying mathematics, graphical chart analysis, economics, business knowledge, human behavioural psychology and common sense to his investment methods and decisions.

He also believes that more people would invest in shares if only they understood more about them, how to analyse and buy them and how to manage the risks involved. This is the driving force behind "How To Invest In Shares" and SharesCoach.com and is the reason he started those businesses.